Entrepreneurship in the Digital Landscape

C. P. Kumar
Reiki Healer
Roorkee - 247667, India

Disclaimer

While every effort has been made to ensure the accuracy and completeness of the content in this book, the author cannot guarantee that the information contained herein is error-free, up-to-date, or suitable for every individual circumstance.

The author shall not be held liable or responsible for any errors or omissions in the content of the book, nor for any damages, or losses that may arise from any actions taken based upon the suggestions or contents presented in the book.

Readers are advised to use their own judgment and discretion in applying the information provided in this book, and to consult with qualified professionals before taking any action based on the contents of this book. The author disclaims any and all liability or responsibility for any actions taken or not taken based on the information contained in this book.

DEDICATION

To the visionaries who dared to pioneer, the dreamers who saw opportunities where others saw obstacles, and the first-generation entrepreneurs who embarked on a journey that not only transformed their lives but also set a course for others to follow. This dedication is a tribute to your resilience, innovation, and unwavering spirit.

May your stories inspire the next generation of digital entrepreneurs to navigate uncharted waters, embrace the challenges, and build legacies that transcend the boundaries of the digital landscape. Your commitment to forging new paths and embracing the evolving entrepreneurial mindset has paved the way for a future where innovation knows no bounds.

Here's to the pioneers, the risk-takers, and the builders of tomorrow's digital enterprises. Your journey, encapsulated in the chapters of this book, serves as a testament to the transformative power of entrepreneurship in the digital era.

With admiration and respect,

C. P. Kumar

CONTENTS

PREFACE

In the dynamic landscape of modern entrepreneurship, this book serves as a compass for those embarking on the exhilarating journey of building businesses in the era of pixels and algorithms.

Chapter by chapter, the narrative unfolds, starting with an exploration of the unique challenges and opportunities that define the initiation of a familial legacy. We delve into the path of those who dare to be the first in their lineage to tread the entrepreneurial road.

The mental acumen that separates successful digital-age entrepreneurs from the rest takes center stage in the following chapters. As we progress, the book underscores the importance of adaptability in an ever-evolving landscape.

The exploration takes a deep dive into the intricacies of online business and the dynamic role of digital marketing. Chapters guide readers in establishing a robust online brand and leveraging the power of search engine optimization.

The journey continues with insights into social media marketing, the artistry of content marketing, and the mastery of email marketing - each chapter unveiling the critical skills and strategies necessary for success in the digital domain.

Beyond the digital canvas, the book emphasizes the holistic development of entrepreneurs, offering practical guidance on communication skills essential for creating an influential presence in the business world.

In the latter part of the book, we delve into the nitty-gritty of strategic planning, providing readers with a comprehensive framework for crafting effective campaigns. Addressing current hurdles faced by digital entrepreneurs and exploring innovative solutions and emerging trends follow.

Finally, the book concludes by envisioning the landscape that awaits the next wave of pioneers. It offers a forward-looking perspective on trends and possibilities, providing readers with the foresight to navigate the ever-evolving intersection of entrepreneurship and the digital landscape.

This book is more than a guide; it is an immersive journey into the heart of modern business. Whether you are a first-generation entrepreneur carving your path or a seasoned professional adapting to the digital age, the insights within these pages will empower you to thrive in the exciting world of entrepreneurship. Welcome to a roadmap for success in the digital era.

C. P. Kumar
Reiki Healer
Former Scientist 'G', National Institute of Hydrology
Roorkee - 247667, India
Web: https://www.angelfire.com/nh/cpkumar/virgo.html

Chapter 1. The Genesis of a First-Generation Entrepreneur

Introduction

Entrepreneurship in the Digital Landscape has witnessed a paradigm shift, with individuals from diverse backgrounds and family histories venturing into the uncharted territory of business ownership. One fascinating aspect of this evolution is the rise of first-generation entrepreneurs who are not only pioneers in the digital era but also trailblazers in their families. This article delves into the journey of becoming a first-generation entrepreneur, exploring the unique challenges and opportunities that come with being the inaugural entrepreneur in one's family.

The Seed of Ambition

Every entrepreneurial journey begins with a spark of ambition, often fueled by a combination of personal passion, a desire for autonomy, and a recognition of untapped opportunities. First-generation entrepreneurs typically find themselves drawn to the allure of creating something from nothing, building a legacy that goes beyond the confines of traditional career paths. This seed of ambition is often sown in the fertile grounds of curiosity and a relentless pursuit of excellence.

The Family Legacy

Unlike subsequent generations of entrepreneurs who may inherit a family business, the first-generation entrepreneur is tasked with crafting a legacy from scratch. This absence of a familial entrepreneurial history can be both liberating and daunting. Liberating because there are no predefined expectations or rigid structures to adhere to, and daunting because the entrepreneur has to forge their own path, often navigating uncharted waters without the safety net of prior experience.

Educational Landscape and Skill Acquisition

First-generation entrepreneurs frequently encounter a unique set of challenges in the realm of education and skill acquisition. Without the advantage of a family business to step into, they must proactively seek out relevant education and practical experience. This might involve pursuing non-traditional educational paths, attending workshops, and networking within their chosen industry. The digital landscape provides a plethora of resources, from online courses to mentorship programs, allowing these entrepreneurs to bridge the knowledge gap and equip themselves for the journey ahead.

Overcoming Skepticism and Resistance

The decision to embark on an entrepreneurial journey is often met with skepticism and resistance, especially in families where the tradition has been to follow established career paths. First-generation entrepreneurs may find themselves swimming against the tide of conventional wisdom, facing questions from family members about the stability and feasibility of their chosen path. This skepticism can be a significant emotional hurdle, necessitating a blend of resilience and effective communication skills to articulate and defend their vision.

Financial Challenges

For many first-generation entrepreneurs, the lack of a financial cushion or family wealth to fall back on can be a major hurdle. Funding a startup in the digital era requires capital not only for product development but also for marketing, technology, and talent acquisition. Without the luxury of family resources, these entrepreneurs often explore creative avenues such as crowdfunding, angel investors, or bootstrapping to fund their ventures. The financial challenges they face, however, also foster a sense of fiscal discipline and resourcefulness.

Crowdfunding: A method of raising funds for a project or venture by collecting small contributions from a large number of people, typically via online platforms.

Angel investors: Individuals who provide financial backing to early-stage startups or entrepreneurs in exchange for equity in the company.

Bootstrapping: The process of self-funding and building a business without external capital or minimal external resources, relying on personal savings and revenue generation.

Navigating the Digital Landscape

The digital landscape offers unprecedented opportunities for entrepreneurs, but it also presents a steep learning curve. First-generation entrepreneurs must familiarize themselves with rapidly evolving technologies, digital marketing strategies, and e-commerce platforms. The ability to adapt and stay ahead of technological trends becomes crucial for success. Unlike entrepreneurs with family legacies, these pioneers are not constrained by preexisting systems, allowing them to embrace innovation and experiment with unconventional approaches.

Building a Support System

In the absence of a family legacy in entrepreneurship, first-generation entrepreneurs often seek support from alternative networks. Mentorship becomes a valuable resource, offering guidance, insights, and a sounding board for ideas. Networking within the entrepreneurial community, both online and offline, becomes an essential part of their journey. Building relationships with fellow entrepreneurs, industry experts, and potential collaborators can open doors to opportunities and provide a sense of community in an otherwise solitary pursuit.

Cultural and Social Dynamics

The cultural and social dynamics surrounding entrepreneurship vary significantly across regions and communities. First-generation entrepreneurs may find themselves challenging societal norms and expectations, especially in cultures where traditional career paths are highly revered. Breaking away from conventional expectations can be a delicate balance, requiring diplomacy and a strong sense of purpose. Navigating the intersection of cultural values and entrepreneurial pursuits adds an additional layer of complexity to the journey.

The Legacy of Resilience

Despite the challenges, first-generation entrepreneurs forge a legacy of resilience. The ability to weather setbacks, pivot when necessary, and persist in the face of adversity becomes a hallmark of their entrepreneurial journey. This resilience is not only a personal attribute but also a key component of the legacy they pass on to future generations. The first-generation entrepreneur sets the tone for a family legacy in entrepreneurship, establishing a tradition of courage, innovation, and the pursuit of one's passions.

Conclusion

The genesis of a first-generation entrepreneur in the digital landscape is a story of courage, determination, and resilience. These pioneers, unburdened by familial expectations, navigate uncharted territories, leveraging the opportunities presented by the digital era. From overcoming skepticism and financial challenges to building a support system and navigating cultural dynamics, their journey is marked by both unique challenges and unprecedented opportunities. As they leave their imprint on the entrepreneurial landscape, first-generation entrepreneurs lay the foundation for a family legacy that transcends traditional career paths, inspiring future generations to pursue their passions and create their own paths in the digital world.

Introduction

In the ever-evolving realm of Entrepreneurship in the Digital Landscape, success is not merely contingent on technological prowess but also on the entrepreneur's mindset. The mindset of a first-generation entrepreneur plays a pivotal role in navigating the challenges and seizing the opportunities that the digital age presents. This article explores the entrepreneurial mindset and the distinctive qualities that set successful first-generation entrepreneurs apart in the dynamic and competitive digital landscape.

Visionary Thinking

At the heart of the entrepreneurial mindset lies visionary thinking. Successful first-generation entrepreneurs possess the ability to envision a future that transcends the current landscape. They don't merely react to market trends; instead, they proactively shape and redefine those trends. In the digital age, where innovation is rapid, having a visionary outlook allows entrepreneurs to spot opportunities, anticipate shifts, and position themselves ahead of the curve.

Risk-Taking and Adaptability

The digital landscape is inherently volatile, demanding a willingness to take risks and adapt to constant change. First-generation entrepreneurs, unburdened by the weight of tradition, often exhibit a remarkable capacity for risk-taking. They embrace uncertainty, viewing it not as a hindrance but as an inherent part of the entrepreneurial journey. The ability to adapt to evolving technologies, market dynamics, and consumer behaviors is a key trait that distinguishes successful entrepreneurs in the digital age.

Resilience in the Face of Failure

Failure is an inevitable companion on the entrepreneurial journey, especially in the digital landscape where rapid experimentation is the norm. First-generation entrepreneurs confront setbacks with resilience, viewing failures not as insurmountable obstacles but as valuable learning experiences. The ability to bounce back from adversity, iterate on shortcomings, and persevere in the face of challenges is a hallmark of the entrepreneurial mindset that sets successful individuals apart.

Technological Fluency

In the digital age, technological fluency is not a luxury but a necessity for entrepreneurs. Successful first-generation entrepreneurs exhibit a deep understanding of digital technologies relevant to their industry. Whether it's leveraging data analytics, artificial intelligence, or blockchain, these entrepreneurs are adept at incorporating cutting-edge technologies into their business models. This fluency enables them to innovate, optimize processes, and stay competitive in an ever-evolving digital landscape.

Customer-Centric Approach

The digital landscape has transformed the way businesses interact with their customers. Successful first-generation entrepreneurs recognize the importance of a customer-centric approach. They leverage digital tools to gather insights, engage with their audience, and tailor their products or services to meet evolving customer needs. Building strong customer relationships in the digital age involves not only delivering value but also fostering a genuine connection with the target audience.

Continuous Learning and Curiosity

The digital landscape is characterized by rapid advancements and constant evolution. Successful first-generation entrepreneurs exhibit a thirst for knowledge and a commitment to continuous learning. They are curious, proactive learners who stay abreast of industry trends, emerging technologies, and market dynamics. The ability to adapt and evolve in the digital age requires a mindset that embraces learning as an ongoing process, ensuring that entrepreneurs remain at the forefront of innovation.

Entrepreneurial Networking

In the digital age, entrepreneurship is not a solitary pursuit. Successful first-generation entrepreneurs recognize the power of networking and collaboration. They actively engage with other entrepreneurs, industry experts, and mentors in both physical and digital spaces. Entrepreneurial networking provides valuable insights, opens doors to partnerships, and fosters a sense of community. This collaborative mindset enhances an entrepreneur's ability to navigate challenges and capitalize on opportunities in the digital landscape.

Results-Driven Focus

In the digital landscape, where metrics and analytics play a crucial role, successful first-generation entrepreneurs are results-driven. They set clear goals, measure progress, and make data-informed decisions. The ability to interpret and leverage data analytics allows them to optimize strategies, enhance efficiency, and make informed choices that contribute to the growth and sustainability of their ventures.

Agility and Innovation

The digital age rewards agility and innovation. First-generation entrepreneurs who thrive in this landscape possess the ability to pivot quickly in response to market shifts. They are not wedded to rigid plans but rather embrace an iterative approach, experimenting with new ideas and adapting their strategies based on feedback and evolving trends. This agility allows them to stay ahead of competitors and capitalize on emerging opportunities in the dynamic digital environment.

Long-Term Vision and Sustainable Growth

While the digital landscape often encourages rapid growth, successful first-generation entrepreneurs maintain a long-term vision for their ventures. They focus not only on short-term gains but also on building sustainable, scalable businesses. This forward-looking mindset involves strategic planning, responsible resource allocation, and a commitment to ethical business practices that contribute to the long-term success and impact of the entrepreneurial venture.

Conclusion

The entrepreneurial mindset in the digital landscape is a multifaceted attribute that sets successful first-generation entrepreneurs apart. Visionary thinking, risk-taking, resilience, technological fluency, customer-centricity, continuous learning, entrepreneurial networking, results-driven focus, agility, and a commitment to long-term vision collectively form the foundation of this mindset. In a landscape characterized by rapid change and intense competition, the entrepreneurial mindset becomes the compass that guides first-generation entrepreneurs through the complexities of the digital age, helping them not only survive but thrive in the ever-evolving entrepreneurial ecosystem.

Introduction

Entrepreneurship in the Digital Landscape is more than a mere convergence of business and technology - it's a transformative journey reshaping the very essence of how ventures are conceived, operated, and scaled. In this exploration of Entrepreneurship in the Digital Era, we delve into the symbiotic relationship between entrepreneurs and the digital landscape, emphasizing the pivotal role of adaptability in navigating the ever-changing terrain of the digital age.

The Digital Landscape Redefined

The digital era has ushered in a paradigm shift in the way businesses operate. From the rise of e-commerce and the advent of social media to the pervasive influence of data analytics and artificial intelligence, entrepreneurs find themselves navigating a landscape that is not only dynamic but also interconnected in unprecedented ways. The digital canvas provides a vast array of tools and platforms, opening new frontiers for innovation, collaboration, and market reach.

Digital Entrepreneurship: Breaking Barriers

Digital entrepreneurship has dismantled traditional barriers to entry, democratizing access to markets and resources. Entrepreneurs no longer require massive capital or extensive physical infrastructure to launch and grow their ventures. The digital landscape allows for lean, agile startups to compete on a global scale, fostering an environment where innovation and ideas take precedence over traditional hierarchies and legacy systems.

The Role of Adaptability

Adaptability emerges as a linchpin in the success of entrepreneurs navigating the digital era. The pace of technological evolution and the fluidity of market dynamics demand a mindset that is not only open to change but actively embraces it. Entrepreneurs must be willing to pivot, iterate, and reinvent their strategies in response to emerging trends, consumer behaviors, and technological advancements.

Harnessing Technological Innovation

Entrepreneurs in the digital era are tasked with not only staying abreast of technological innovations but also harnessing them to their advantage. The ability to integrate emerging technologies, such as blockchain, Internet of Things (IoT), and machine learning, into business models is a distinguishing factor. Those who successfully leverage these tools gain a competitive edge, driving efficiency, enhancing customer experiences, and creating new revenue streams.

Digital Marketing and Brand Building

The digital landscape has revolutionized marketing, offering entrepreneurs powerful tools to reach and engage with their target audiences. From social media platforms to search engine optimization (SEO) strategies, entrepreneurs must navigate the intricacies of digital marketing to establish and amplify their brand presence. Crafting compelling digital narratives, building online communities, and fostering brand loyalty are critical components of success in the digital era.

Data-Driven Decision-Making

In the digital era, data is a currency of immense value. Entrepreneurs have access to a wealth of information that can inform strategic decisions, guide product development, and optimize operations. Those who embrace a data-driven approach gain actionable insights, enabling them to respond to market demands, personalize user experiences, and refine their business strategies with precision.

E-Commerce and the Global Market

E-commerce has transcended borders, allowing entrepreneurs to tap into a global market with relative ease. The digital landscape facilitates seamless cross-border transactions, opening new avenues for growth and diversification. Entrepreneurs who adeptly navigate international markets can capitalize on diverse consumer demographics, adapt to cultural nuances, and position their ventures for sustained success on a global scale.

Remote Work and Virtual Collaboration

The digital era has redefined the workplace, with remote work and virtual collaboration becoming integral aspects of modern entrepreneurship. Entrepreneurs harness digital communication tools, project management platforms, and collaborative technologies to build and manage teams dispersed across geographical boundaries. Adapting to the remote work paradigm enables entrepreneurs to access diverse talent pools and foster a culture of innovation and flexibility.

Cybersecurity Challenges

While the digital landscape presents unparalleled opportunities, it also introduces new challenges, particularly in the realm of cybersecurity. Entrepreneurs must navigate the complex terrain of safeguarding sensitive data, protecting against cyber threats, and ensuring the trust and security of their digital transactions. The ability to implement robust cybersecurity measures becomes imperative for the long-term sustainability of digital ventures.

Environmental Sustainability and Corporate Responsibility

In the digital era, entrepreneurship goes beyond profit margins to encompass environmental sustainability and corporate responsibility. Entrepreneurs are increasingly scrutinized for their ethical practices, environmental impact, and commitment to social causes. Adapting to this shift in consumer expectations and integrating sustainability into business models is not only a strategic advantage but also a reflection of an entrepreneur's responsiveness to societal concerns.

Conclusion

Entrepreneurship in the Digital Era is a dynamic and multifaceted journey, where the ability to adapt is as crucial as innovation itself. The digital landscape offers a canvas of opportunities, but it requires entrepreneurs to be agile, forward-thinking, and responsive to change. Navigating the terrain of the digital age involves not only harnessing technological advancements but also cultivating a mindset that thrives on adaptability, resilience, and a commitment to continuous learning. As entrepreneurs embark on this transformative journey, they become architects of change, shaping the future of business in the digital landscape.

Introduction

In the realm of Entrepreneurship in the Digital Landscape, the online business landscape stands as a testament to the transformative power of the digital era. This article explores the intricacies of navigating the online business terrain, delving into the evolving role of digital marketing in shaping the success of ventures in the digital age.

The Proliferation of Online Business

The digital revolution has given rise to a thriving online business landscape, where entrepreneurs can establish, grow, and scale ventures with unprecedented ease. E-commerce platforms, online marketplaces, and digital storefronts have become the norm, providing entrepreneurs with a global reach and 24/7 accessibility. The barriers to entry have been significantly lowered, allowing innovative ideas to flourish and reshaping the traditional notions of commerce.

Building a Digital Presence

Central to the success of any online business is the establishment of a robust digital presence. Entrepreneurs must navigate the intricacies of creating and optimizing websites, ensuring user-friendly interfaces, and developing engaging content. The digital storefront serves as the virtual storefront, making the first impression on potential customers. Entrepreneurs who invest in creating a compelling and responsive online presence lay the foundation for customer trust and brand loyalty.

Digital Marketing Strategies

In the online business landscape, digital marketing is the linchpin that connects businesses with their target audiences. Entrepreneurs must craft comprehensive digital marketing strategies that encompass various channels, including social media, search engine optimization (SEO), content marketing, email campaigns, and online advertising. The ability to navigate this complex web of digital marketing tools is crucial for driving brand awareness, customer acquisition, and revenue growth.

Social Media: The Hub of Engagement

Social media has emerged as a dynamic hub for online business engagement. Entrepreneurs leverage platforms like Facebook, Instagram, Twitter, and LinkedIn to connect with their audience, build brand identity, and foster community. Navigating the social media landscape involves not only crafting engaging content but also understanding the nuances of each platform, utilizing analytics, and adapting strategies to changing algorithms.

Search Engine Optimization (SEO)

In the online business landscape, visibility is paramount, and SEO is the compass that guides entrepreneurs to the top of search engine results. Navigating the intricacies of SEO involves optimizing website content, building high-quality backlinks, and staying abreast of search engine algorithms. Entrepreneurs who master the art of SEO enhance their online visibility, driving organic traffic and establishing a strong foundation for digital success.

Content is King

Content marketing remains a cornerstone of online business strategies. Entrepreneurs must navigate the creation of high-quality, relevant, and valuable content that resonates with their target audience. Whether through blog posts, videos, podcasts, or infographics, compelling content not only attracts and engages customers but also enhances a brand's authority in the digital landscape.

Email Campaigns and Automation

Email remains a powerful tool in the online business arsenal. Entrepreneurs navigate the landscape of email marketing by creating targeted campaigns, personalized messaging, and automated workflows. Building and nurturing an email subscriber base allows entrepreneurs to establish direct communication channels with their audience, fostering customer relationships and driving conversions.

E-Commerce Platforms and Payment Gateways

For online businesses, choosing the right e-commerce platform and payment gateway is critical. Navigating the diverse options involves considerations of user experience, security, scalability, and integration capabilities. Entrepreneurs must ensure a seamless and secure online shopping experience for customers, from product browsing to checkout, to instill confidence and encourage repeat business.

Customer Analytics and Data Insights

In the online business landscape, data is a valuable asset. Entrepreneurs navigate the world of customer analytics and data insights to understand consumer behavior, preferences, and trends. Utilizing tools like Google Analytics and customer relationship management (CRM) systems enables entrepreneurs to make data-driven decisions, optimize marketing strategies, and tailor products or services to meet evolving customer needs.

Cybersecurity and Trust

As online businesses thrive, cybersecurity becomes a paramount concern. Entrepreneurs must navigate the landscape of cybersecurity, implementing robust measures to protect customer data, secure transactions, and safeguard the integrity of their online platforms. Building trust in the digital realm involves not only delivering quality products or services but also ensuring the security and privacy of customer information.

Conclusion

Navigating the online business landscape requires a multifaceted approach that encompasses digital marketing, e-commerce platforms, customer analytics, and cybersecurity. Entrepreneurs in the digital age must not only embrace the opportunities presented by the online business terrain but also navigate its complexities with finesse. As the digital landscape continues to evolve, entrepreneurs who master the art of online business navigation position themselves to not only survive but thrive in the dynamic and competitive digital era. The online business landscape stands as a testament to the transformative power of the digital era, reshaping the very essence of how ventures are conceived, operated, and scaled.

27

Introduction

In the ever-evolving landscape of Entrepreneurship in the Digital Era, the ascent of online marketing has been a transformative force. This article traces the historical evolution of online marketing, unraveling its roots and exploring its profound significance in contemporary business. From its humble beginnings to its current status as a cornerstone of digital entrepreneurship, the rise of online marketing is a compelling narrative that reflects the dynamic nature of the digital landscape.

Origins of Online Marketing

The inception of online marketing can be traced back to the early days of the internet. As the World Wide Web emerged in the 1990s, businesses recognized the potential of reaching a global audience through digital channels. Banner ads, the pioneers of online advertising, made their debut, gracing the screens of early websites. These static, clickable images marked the humble beginnings of a revolution that would redefine the way businesses connect with consumers.

The Dot-Com Boom and E-Commerce

The late 1990s witnessed the Dot-Com Boom, a period of unprecedented growth in internet-based businesses. E-commerce platforms emerged, enabling entrepreneurs to sell products and services online. The landscape of online marketing expanded alongside e-commerce, with businesses experimenting with new ways to attract and engage digital audiences. This era laid the foundation for the symbiotic relationship between online marketing and the digital marketplace.

Search Engine Optimization (SEO) Emerges

As the internet became a bustling marketplace, the need for visibility in search engine results became paramount. The late 1990s and early 2000s saw the birth of Search Engine Optimization (SEO), a practice aimed at optimizing websites to rank higher in search engine listings. Entrepreneurs began navigating the complexities of keywords, meta tags, and link-building to enhance their online visibility - a trend that continues to shape digital marketing strategies today.

Pay-Per-Click (PPC) Advertising

In the early 2000s, Pay-Per-Click (PPC) advertising emerged as a game-changer in online marketing. Google AdWords, launched in 2000, allowed businesses to bid on keywords and pay only when users clicked on their ads. This model not only revolutionized digital advertising but also provided a measurable and cost-effective way for entrepreneurs to drive targeted traffic to their websites.

Social Media Revolutionizes Marketing

The mid-2000s witnessed the meteoric rise of social media platforms, ushering in a new era of online marketing. Platforms like Facebook, Twitter, and later, Instagram, provided businesses with unprecedented opportunities to engage with their audiences on a personal level. Entrepreneurs navigated this social landscape, leveraging user-generated content, influencer marketing, and viral campaigns to amplify their brand messages.

Content Marketing Takes Center Stage

As consumers became more discerning, entrepreneurs recognized the need for valuable and relevant content. Content marketing emerged as a powerful strategy, with businesses creating blog posts, articles, videos, and infographics to engage and educate their target audience. Navigating the landscape of content marketing involved storytelling, building brand narratives, and establishing thought leadership - a trend that continues to shape online marketing strategies.

Mobile Marketing and the Rise of Apps

The proliferation of smartphones in the late 2000s marked a pivotal moment in online marketing. Entrepreneurs adapted their strategies to reach audiences on mobile devices, leading to the rise of mobile marketing. Mobile apps became a prominent channel for engagement, with businesses navigating app development, in-app advertising, and location-based marketing to connect with consumers in real-time.

Video Marketing Dominates

The 2010s witnessed the ascendance of video marketing as one of the most compelling forms of online content. Platforms like YouTube became integral to online marketing strategies, with entrepreneurs navigating the creation of engaging video content to tell their brand stories. Live streaming, 360-degree videos (video recordings that capture a panoramic view of an environment in all directions, allowing viewers to explore the entire surroundings by rotating the perspective during playback), and interactive content added new dimensions to the online marketing landscape.

Personalization and Data-Driven Marketing

In contemporary online marketing, personalization has become a cornerstone. Entrepreneurs navigate the collection and analysis of data to tailor marketing messages to individual preferences. Email campaigns, targeted ads, and product recommendations are finely tuned through data-driven insights, enhancing the customer experience and driving conversion rates.

The Future of Online Marketing: Artificial Intelligence and Beyond

As we navigate the current digital landscape, the future of online marketing is being shaped by emerging technologies, most notably, artificial intelligence (AI). Machine learning algorithms analyze vast datasets to predict consumer behavior, automate marketing processes, and deliver personalized experiences. Entrepreneurs are navigating the integration of AI into their marketing strategies, ushering in a new era of efficiency and innovation.

Conclusion

The rise of online marketing is a compelling narrative that unfolds across the tapestry of the digital landscape. From the early days of banner ads to the current era of artificial intelligence, entrepreneurs have navigated a dynamic and ever-evolving terrain. Online marketing has become not just a tool but a fundamental aspect of contemporary business, shaping how entrepreneurs connect with their audiences, build brand identities, and drive growth in the digital era. As we continue to traverse the digital landscape, the story of online marketing remains one of adaptation, innovation, and the relentless pursuit of effective strategies that resonate with the ever-changing expectations of digital consumers.

Introduction

In the dynamic landscape of Entrepreneurship in the Digital Era, crafting a robust digital presence is not just a strategic move - it's a necessity. As businesses increasingly migrate to the online realm, entrepreneurs find themselves navigating a landscape where the strength of their digital presence can make or break their success. This article explores the essential strategies for establishing a powerful online presence and building a brand in the ever-evolving digital space.

Understanding the Digital Landscape

Before embarking on the journey of crafting a digital presence, entrepreneurs must first comprehend the nuances of the digital landscape. The online realm is multifaceted, encompassing websites, social media platforms, search engines, e-commerce, and more. Navigating this landscape involves a holistic understanding of how these elements interact and influence each other to shape the overall digital identity of a brand.

Defining Your Brand Identity

At the core of crafting a digital presence is a clear and compelling brand identity. Entrepreneurs must articulate their brand's values, mission, and unique selling propositions. This involves more than just designing a visually appealing logo; it's about defining the personality of the brand, the tone of communication, and the emotions it aims to evoke. A well-defined brand identity serves as the foundation upon which a powerful digital presence is built.

Building a User-Friendly Website

In the digital landscape, a business's website is often the first point of interaction with potential customers. Crafting a user-friendly website is paramount. Entrepreneurs must ensure that their website is easy to navigate, mobile-responsive, and optimized for search engines. Clear and concise messaging, compelling visuals, and intuitive navigation contribute to a positive user experience, encouraging visitors to explore further and engage with the brand.

Leveraging Social Media Platforms

Social media has become a cornerstone of digital presence. Entrepreneurs navigate platforms like Facebook, Instagram, Twitter, LinkedIn, and others to connect with their audience. Crafting a strong social media presence involves consistent branding across platforms, regular content sharing, engagement with followers, and leveraging features like stories and live videos. Entrepreneurs must adapt their strategies to the unique dynamics of each platform, understanding the preferences and behaviors of their target audience.

Content is King: Blogging and Beyond

Compelling and valuable content lies at the heart of a strong digital presence. Entrepreneurs navigate content creation by incorporating a blog into their website. Blogging not only provides a platform to showcase industry expertise but also contributes to search engine optimization (SEO). Beyond blogging, entrepreneurs explore diverse content formats such as videos, infographics, podcasts, and interactive content to engage their audience and share their brand story.

Search Engine Optimization (SEO) Strategies

Navigating the digital landscape involves understanding the significance of search engines in driving organic traffic. Entrepreneurs employ SEO strategies to optimize their websites for search engine algorithms. This includes keyword research, on-page optimization, link-building, and technical SEO elements. A well-executed SEO strategy enhances a brand's visibility, driving organic traffic and establishing credibility in the digital space.

Email Marketing Campaigns

Email marketing remains a powerful tool for engaging and nurturing a brand's audience. Entrepreneurs craft email campaigns that deliver personalized and valuable content directly to subscribers. Navigating email marketing involves segmenting audiences, creating compelling email copy, and leveraging automation for timely and relevant communication. Successful email campaigns contribute to building and maintaining strong relationships with customers.

E-Commerce Integration

For businesses involved in selling products or services, navigating the digital landscape requires the integration of e-commerce solutions. Entrepreneurs establish an online storefront, leveraging platforms like Shopify, WooCommerce, or Magento. Crafting a seamless e-commerce experience involves optimizing product pages, streamlining the checkout process, and ensuring secure payment gateways. The ability to adapt to evolving e-commerce trends contributes to a brand's success in the digital marketplace.

Online Reputation Management

In the digital era, a brand's reputation is shaped not only by its messaging but also by the perceptions and feedback of customers. Entrepreneurs navigate online reputation management by actively monitoring reviews, responding to customer feedback, and addressing concerns transparently. Building and maintaining a positive online reputation is essential for establishing trust and credibility in the digital space.

Analytics and Data-Driven Decision-Making

Navigating the digital landscape is not a one-size-fits-all endeavor. Entrepreneurs must embrace analytics and data-driven insights to understand the effectiveness of their digital strategies. Tools like Google Analytics provide valuable data on website traffic, user behavior, and conversion rates. By interpreting these insights, entrepreneurs can refine their strategies, optimize campaigns, and make informed decisions to continuously improve their digital presence.

Conclusion

Crafting a digital presence is a dynamic and ongoing process that requires adaptability, creativity, and a deep understanding of the digital landscape. Entrepreneurs must navigate websites, social media, content creation, SEO, email marketing, e-commerce, and online reputation management to build a cohesive and impactful brand in the digital space. The strategies outlined in this article serve as a roadmap for entrepreneurs seeking to establish a strong and enduring digital presence, ensuring that their brand resonates with audiences in the ever-evolving landscape of Entrepreneurship in the Digital Era.

Introduction

In the expansive landscape of Entrepreneurship in the Digital Era, one tool stands out as a game-changer for online businesses - Search Engine Optimization (SEO). This article delves into the fundamentals of SEO, examining how it can be a transformative force for entrepreneurs navigating the competitive and dynamic digital landscape.

Understanding the Fundamentals of SEO

At its core, Search Engine Optimization is the practice of optimizing digital content to enhance its visibility and ranking on search engine results pages (SERPs). The fundamentals of SEO revolve around aligning website content with the algorithms used by search engines, primarily Google, to ensure that a business's online presence is not only discovered but also prioritized by users searching for relevant information.

The Importance of Keyword Research

Central to any successful SEO strategy is the meticulous process of keyword research. Entrepreneurs must navigate the landscape of user intent, industry trends, and competitive analysis to identify the keywords and phrases their target audience is likely to use when searching for products or services. By understanding these keywords, businesses can tailor their content to align with user queries, enhancing their chances of ranking higher on SERPs.

On-Page Optimization

On-page optimization involves fine-tuning individual web pages to improve their relevance to specific keywords. Entrepreneurs navigate the intricacies of meta tags, headers, and content structure to signal to search engines what each page is about. Crafting compelling and informative content that incorporates relevant keywords naturally is a balancing act that ensures both search engine visibility and a positive user experience.

Technical SEO Elements

Technical SEO focuses on optimizing the backend infrastructure of a website to improve its crawlability, indexability, and overall performance. Entrepreneurs navigate technical SEO by addressing issues such as website speed, mobile responsiveness, and site architecture. A technically sound website not only provides a better user experience but also earns favor with search engines, contributing to higher rankings.

Off-Page Optimization: Building Backlinks

Off-page optimization, specifically building high-quality backlinks, is a critical aspect of SEO. Entrepreneurs navigate the landscape of backlink acquisition by earning links from reputable and relevant websites. Backlinks serve as endorsements, signaling to search engines that a website is authoritative and trustworthy. Navigating the complexities of ethical link-building contributes to a website's overall SEO success.

Local SEO for Small Businesses

For local businesses, local SEO is a game-changer. Entrepreneurs navigate this aspect of SEO by optimizing their online presence for location-specific searches. This involves creating and optimizing Google My Business profiles, acquiring local citations, and encouraging customer reviews. Local SEO ensures that businesses appear in local search results, making them more accessible to potential customers in their geographic vicinity.

Content is Key: The Role of Quality Content in SEO

In the SEO landscape, content is not merely a means to an end; it's a foundational element. Entrepreneurs navigate content creation by developing high-quality, relevant, and engaging content that addresses the needs and interests of their target audience. Search engines prioritize content that provides value to users, making quality content a key driver of SEO success.

User Experience and SEO

User experience (UX) is intricately tied to SEO success. UX encompasses the overall interaction and satisfaction a person has while using a product, service, or system. Entrepreneurs navigate the landscape of UX by ensuring that their websites are easy to navigate, aesthetically pleasing, and optimized for various devices. Search engines consider factors such as bounce rates and dwell time when ranking websites, making a positive UX crucial for maintaining high rankings.

The Role of Social Media in SEO

While social media doesn't have a direct impact on search engine rankings, it plays an indirect role in SEO success. Entrepreneurs navigate social media by using these platforms to share and promote their content, fostering brand awareness, and potentially earning backlinks. The social signals generated by social media activity can contribute to a brand's online visibility and authority.

Measuring and Adapting with Analytics

The success of any SEO strategy hinges on the ability to measure its effectiveness and adapt accordingly. Entrepreneurs navigate the landscape of analytics tools, such as Google Analytics, to track website performance, user behavior, and the impact of SEO efforts. By interpreting data insights, entrepreneurs can refine their strategies, identify areas for improvement, and stay agile in the ever-evolving digital landscape.

Conclusion

The SEO advantage is a formidable force that empowers entrepreneurs in the digital landscape. By understanding the fundamentals of SEO and navigating its intricacies, businesses can enhance their online visibility, connect with their target audience, and outperform competitors in the digital space. SEO is not a one-time endeavor but an ongoing process that requires adaptability, strategic thinking, and a commitment to delivering valuable content and experiences to users. For entrepreneurs looking to thrive in the digital era, embracing the power of SEO is not just an option - it's a strategic imperative that can position their businesses for sustained success in the competitive digital landscape.

Introduction

In the ever-evolving landscape of Entrepreneurship in the Digital Era, becoming an SEO expert is a transformative journey. As businesses increasingly rely on online visibility, the role of SEO consultants becomes crucial. This article delves into the skills and knowledge required to excel as an SEO expert, exploring the intricacies of the digital landscape and the ever-changing algorithms that shape search engine results.

The Foundation: Understanding Search Engine Basics

Becoming an SEO expert begins with a solid understanding of how search engines work. Entrepreneurs must navigate the fundamentals of search engine algorithms, crawling, indexing, and ranking. This foundational knowledge lays the groundwork for effective SEO strategies and informed decision-making.

Keyword Research Mastery

A key skill for an SEO expert is the ability to conduct comprehensive keyword research. Navigating the landscape of user intent, industry trends, and competitor analysis, SEO experts identify keywords that align with a business's objectives. This skill ensures that content is optimized for the terms users are searching for, enhancing a website's visibility on search engine results pages (SERPs).

On-Page Optimization Expertise

The art of on-page optimization involves fine-tuning individual web pages to align with search engine algorithms. SEO experts navigate meta tags, headers, and content structure to optimize each page for specific keywords. Crafting compelling and informative content that seamlessly incorporates relevant keywords is a skill that contributes to both search engine visibility and positive user experiences.

Technical SEO Proficiency

Technical SEO focuses on optimizing the backend infrastructure of a website to improve its crawlability, indexability, and overall performance. Becoming an SEO expert involves navigating technical elements such as website speed, mobile responsiveness, and site architecture. A technically sound website not only enhances user experience but also earns favor with search engines, positively impacting rankings.

Backlink Building Mastery

Off-page optimization, particularly building high-quality backlinks, is a critical aspect of SEO expertise. SEO experts navigate the landscape of ethical link-building by earning endorsements from reputable and relevant websites. These backlinks signal to search engines that a website is authoritative and trustworthy, contributing significantly to higher rankings.

Local SEO Finesse

For an SEO expert, mastering local SEO is essential, especially for businesses targeting specific geographic areas. Navigating local SEO involves optimizing online presence for location-specific searches, creating and optimizing Google My Business profiles, acquiring local citations, and managing customer reviews. Local SEO ensures businesses appear prominently in local search results, connecting them with nearby customers.

Content Creation Prowess

Quality content is at the heart of effective SEO strategies. SEO experts must navigate content creation by developing high-quality, relevant, and engaging content. Beyond traditional text-based content, experts explore diverse formats such as videos, infographics, and interactive content to cater to varied audience preferences and enhance a website's overall appeal.

User Experience Enhancement

User experience (UX) is intricately tied to SEO success. SEO experts navigate the landscape of UX by ensuring websites are easy to navigate, aesthetically pleasing, and optimized for various devices. Positive user experiences contribute to lower bounce rates, increased dwell time, and ultimately, higher rankings on search engines.

Social Media Integration

While not a direct factor in search engine rankings, social media plays an indirect role in SEO success. SEO experts navigate social media platforms strategically, using them to share and promote content, foster brand awareness, and potentially earn backlinks. Social signals generated through social media activity contribute to a brand's online visibility and authority.

Analytics Interpretation

The ability to measure the effectiveness of SEO efforts and adapt strategies accordingly is a hallmark of SEO expertise. SEO experts navigate analytics tools such as Google Analytics to track website performance, user behavior, and the impact of SEO campaigns. Interpreting data insights allows experts to refine strategies, identify areas for improvement, and stay agile in the ever-evolving digital landscape.

Keeping Abreast of Algorithm Changes

The digital landscape is dynamic, and search engine algorithms are in a constant state of evolution. Becoming an SEO expert involves staying informed about algorithm changes and industry trends. Navigating the landscape of algorithm updates requires a commitment to continuous learning, as staying ahead of the curve is essential for devising effective and future-proof SEO strategies.

Adaptability and Continuous Learning

Becoming an SEO expert is not a one-time achievement but an ongoing journey. SEO experts must navigate the ever-changing digital landscape by staying adaptable and committed to continuous learning. The SEO field is dynamic, and strategies that worked yesterday may not be effective tomorrow. An expert's ability to adapt ensures their skills remain relevant and effective in the face of evolving challenges.

Conclusion

Becoming an SEO expert is a multifaceted journey that demands a combination of skills, knowledge, and adaptability. Navigating the digital landscape requires expertise in keyword research, on-page optimization, technical SEO, backlink building, local SEO, content creation, user experience enhancement, social media integration, and analytics interpretation. The role of an SEO expert is further complicated by the continuous evolution of search engine algorithms, making a commitment to continuous learning and adaptability essential. As businesses increasingly recognize the importance of online visibility, SEO experts play a pivotal role in shaping digital success stories in the competitive and dynamic Entrepreneurship in the Digital Era.

Introduction

In the fast-paced realm of Entrepreneurship in the Digital Era, social media marketing stands out as a potent force for businesses aiming to connect with audiences and drive success. This article explores the nuances of leveraging social media marketing, delving into the strategies, challenges, and transformative impact it can have on businesses navigating the dynamic digital landscape.

The Social Media Landscape

Understanding the landscape of social media is the first step in leveraging its marketing potential. Social media platforms, including but not limited to Facebook, Instagram, Twitter, LinkedIn, and TikTok, offer diverse environments for businesses to engage with their target audiences. Navigating this landscape involves recognizing the unique features, user demographics, and content preferences of each platform.

Crafting a Consistent Brand Presence

Leveraging social media for marketing requires entrepreneurs to craft a consistent brand presence across platforms. This involves establishing cohesive visual elements, tone of voice, and messaging that resonate with the brand's identity. Navigating the landscape of brand consistency fosters recognition and trust among audiences, whether they encounter the brand on Facebook, Instagram, or other platforms.

Audience Identification and Targeting

One of the strengths of social media marketing lies in its ability to precisely target specific audiences. Entrepreneurs navigate the landscape of audience identification by utilizing demographic information, interests, and online behavior to tailor their content and advertisements. This targeted approach ensures that marketing efforts reach the right people at the right time, maximizing impact.

Engaging Content Creation

At the heart of successful social media marketing is engaging content. Entrepreneurs navigate the landscape of content creation by developing posts, images, videos, and other media that captivate and resonate with their audience. Crafting content that sparks interest, evokes emotions, and encourages interaction is essential for maintaining an active and engaged social media presence.

Utilizing Paid Advertising

While organic reach is valuable, social media platforms offer robust paid advertising options. Entrepreneurs navigate the landscape of paid advertising by strategically using platforms like Facebook Ads, Instagram Ads, and LinkedIn Ads. Paid advertising allows businesses to extend their reach, target specific demographics, and track the performance of their campaigns with precision.

Building and Nurturing Communities

Social media provides an opportunity to build and nurture communities around a brand. Entrepreneurs navigate the landscape of community building by fostering engagement, responding to comments, and encouraging user-generated content. Creating a sense of belonging and community on social media can lead to brand advocacy and long-term customer loyalty.

Social Media Analytics and Insights

Leveraging social media marketing involves more than just posting content; it requires analyzing performance metrics. Entrepreneurs navigate the landscape of social media analytics to understand the impact of their efforts. Platforms offer insights into reach, engagement, click-through rates, and audience demographics, empowering businesses to refine their strategies based on data-driven decisions.

Influencer Marketing Strategies

In the landscape of social media marketing, influencers can play a pivotal role in amplifying a brand's message. Entrepreneurs navigate influencer marketing by identifying individuals with a significant following and aligning with their audience. Collaborating with influencers provides access to a ready-made audience and adds authenticity to the brand's messaging.

Real-Time Engagement

Social media is inherently real-time, and successful marketing involves navigating the landscape of instant engagement. Entrepreneurs respond to comments, messages, and mentions promptly. Engaging with the audience in real-time not only strengthens the brand-consumer relationship but also demonstrates attentiveness and responsiveness.

Challenges of Social Media Marketing

While social media marketing offers immense opportunities, it comes with its set of challenges. Entrepreneurs navigate the landscape of algorithm changes, platform updates, and evolving consumer behaviors. Staying ahead requires adaptability and a continuous effort to understand the shifting dynamics of the social media landscape.

Crisis Management and Reputation

Navigating the landscape of social media marketing also involves being prepared for potential crises. Negative comments, controversies, or misunderstandings can arise. Entrepreneurs must have effective crisis management strategies in place to address issues promptly and protect their brand's reputation.

Emerging Trends in Social Media Marketing

To leverage social media marketing effectively, entrepreneurs must stay abreast of emerging trends. Navigating the landscape of evolving features, such as live videos, stories, and short-form content, allows businesses to stay relevant and captivate audiences in innovative ways.

Conclusion

Leveraging social media marketing is a dynamic and multifaceted endeavor that requires a strategic approach, creativity, and adaptability. Entrepreneurs navigating the landscape of social media must craft a consistent brand presence, identify and target their audience effectively, create engaging content, and utilize both organic and paid strategies. The challenges and opportunities presented by the social media landscape require entrepreneurs to stay informed, embrace emerging trends, and continuously refine their strategies. In the digital era of Entrepreneurship in the Digital Landscape, social media marketing emerges not only as a promotional tool but as a transformative force that can propel businesses to new heights of success.

Introduction

In the dynamic world of Entrepreneurship in the Digital Era, the art of content marketing stands as a powerful strategy for businesses aiming to build brand authority and connect with their target audiences. This article explores the nuances of content marketing, delving into its transformative impact on businesses navigating the competitive and ever-evolving digital landscape.

Understanding Content Marketing

At its essence, content marketing is the strategic creation and distribution of valuable, relevant, and consistent content to attract and engage a defined audience. Entrepreneurs navigate the landscape of content marketing by crafting narratives that go beyond mere promotion, focusing on delivering information, entertainment, or utility to their target audience.

The Power of Storytelling

Central to the art of content marketing is the ability to tell compelling stories. Entrepreneurs navigate the landscape of storytelling by weaving narratives that resonate with their audience's emotions, experiences, and aspirations. Through stories, businesses can establish a genuine connection, making their brand more relatable and memorable in the minds of consumers.

Aligning Content with Brand Values

Successful content marketing involves aligning the content with the core values and mission of the brand. Entrepreneurs navigate the landscape of brand alignment by ensuring that every piece of content reflects the brand's identity and resonates with its audience. This consistency reinforces brand messaging and fosters a sense of authenticity.

SEO and Content Strategy

Navigating the landscape of content marketing extends to optimizing content for search engines. Entrepreneurs understand the importance of search engine optimization (SEO) and incorporate relevant keywords, meta tags, and other SEO elements into their content. This strategic approach ensures that the content ranks well on search engine results pages, enhancing visibility and reach.

Diverse Content Formats

The art of content marketing involves exploring diverse formats to cater to different audience preferences. Entrepreneurs navigate the landscape of content creation by incorporating blog posts, articles, videos, infographics, podcasts, and interactive content. This variety not only keeps the audience engaged but also expands the reach of the brand across different platforms.

Building Thought Leadership

Content marketing provides a platform for entrepreneurs to establish thought leadership in their industry. Navigating the landscape of thought leadership involves creating content that showcases expertise, insights, and innovative perspectives. By positioning themselves as industry authorities, businesses can attract a loyal audience and gain credibility.

Educational Content

An essential aspect of content marketing is providing value to the audience through educational content. Entrepreneurs navigate the landscape of education by creating content that informs, guides, and solves problems for their audience. Educational content not only positions the brand as a valuable resource but also fosters trust among consumers.

Social Media Amplification

Social media serves as a powerful amplifier for content marketing efforts. Entrepreneurs navigate the landscape of social media by sharing and promoting their content across platforms. Strategic use of social media allows businesses to reach a wider audience, foster engagement, and drive traffic to their owned digital properties.

Interactive and User-Generated Content

Engaging content goes beyond one-way communication. Entrepreneurs navigate the landscape of interactivity by creating quizzes, polls, surveys, and other interactive content that encourages audience participation. User-generated content, such as reviews, testimonials, and social media posts, adds authenticity and builds a sense of community around the brand.

Email Marketing Integration

Content marketing synergizes with email marketing to create a holistic approach. Entrepreneurs navigate the landscape of email marketing by delivering curated content directly to subscribers. Email campaigns, newsletters, and personalized content recommendations contribute to building and maintaining a direct and personalized connection with the audience.

Measuring Content Performance

The effectiveness of content marketing lies in its measurability. Entrepreneurs navigate the landscape of analytics tools to assess content performance. Metrics such as website traffic, engagement rates, conversion rates, and social shares provide valuable insights. Conversion rates refer to the percentage of visitors who take a desired action after interacting with a piece of content. This action could be anything from making a purchase and filling out a form to signing up for a newsletter or downloading a resource. The goal is to track how well the content engages the audience and persuades them to complete the intended objective.

Interpreting these analytics allows businesses to refine their content strategies for optimal impact.

Adapting to Trends and Technologies

The digital landscape is dynamic, and content marketing strategies must evolve accordingly. Entrepreneurs navigate the landscape of emerging trends and technologies, such as artificial intelligence, virtual reality, and interactive storytelling. Adapting to these innovations ensures that content remains relevant and resonant in an ever-changing digital environment.

Conclusion

The art of content marketing is a dynamic and strategic endeavor that empowers entrepreneurs to build brand authority, connect authentically with their audience, and drive business success in the digital landscape. Navigating the landscape involves storytelling, aligning content with brand values, optimizing for SEO, diversifying content formats, and leveraging social media and email marketing. As content marketing continues to evolve, entrepreneurs who master the art will find themselves not just creating content but crafting narratives that inspire, inform, and leave a lasting imprint in the minds of their audience. In the realm of Entrepreneurship in the Digital Landscape, the art of content marketing is not just a tool - it's a transformative force that propels brands towards meaningful connections and sustainable growth.

Introduction

In the intricate realm of Entrepreneurship in the Digital Era, email marketing emerges as a powerful tool for businesses seeking to establish and nurture lasting connections with their audience. This article delves into the art of email marketing, exploring its nuances, strategies, and transformative role in nurturing customer relationships and driving conversions.

Understanding the Essence of Email Marketing

At its core, email marketing is more than just sending promotional messages; it's a strategic approach to connect with the audience on a personal level. Entrepreneurs navigate the landscape of email marketing by leveraging the direct line of communication that emails provide, fostering engagement, and building trust with their subscribers.

Building an Engaged Subscriber List

The foundation of successful email marketing lies in building and maintaining an engaged subscriber list. Entrepreneurs navigate the landscape of list-building by employing ethical tactics such as offering valuable content, exclusive promotions, and incentives to encourage visitors to subscribe. A well-curated subscriber list is essential for reaching an audience genuinely interested in the brand.

Segmentation for Personalized Communication

Navigating the landscape of email marketing involves recognizing the diversity within the subscriber base. Entrepreneurs leverage segmentation to categorize subscribers based on factors such as demographics, purchase history, and behavior. Segmentation enables personalized communication, allowing businesses to send targeted messages that resonate with the specific interests and needs of each segment.

Crafting Compelling and Relevant Content

The heart of email marketing lies in crafting content that is not only compelling but also relevant to the audience. Entrepreneurs navigate the landscape of content creation by developing emails that provide value, whether through informative articles, exclusive offers, or personalized recommendations. The goal is to keep subscribers engaged and eagerly anticipating each communication.

Designing Mobile-Responsive Emails

With the prevalence of mobile devices, entrepreneurs must navigate the landscape of mobile responsiveness in email design. Mobile-friendly emails ensure a seamless experience for subscribers across devices. The layout, images, and call-to-action buttons must be optimized for smaller screens, enhancing accessibility and engagement.

Effective Use of Calls-to-Action (CTAs)

The strategic placement and design of calls-to-action (CTAs) play a pivotal role in the success of email marketing campaigns. Entrepreneurs navigate the landscape of CTAs by creating clear, compelling, and action-oriented buttons that guide subscribers towards desired actions, such as making a purchase, downloading content, or visiting the website.

Automation for Timely and Relevant Communication

Navigating the landscape of email marketing involves the strategic use of automation to deliver timely and relevant messages. Entrepreneurs set up automated workflows triggered by subscriber actions or specific dates. Automation ensures that subscribers receive targeted content, such as welcome emails, abandoned cart reminders, and post-purchase follow-ups, fostering a seamless customer journey.

A/B Testing for Optimization

Entrepreneurs navigate the landscape of optimization through A/B testing. A/B testing is a method of comparing two versions (A and B) of a webpage, email, or other content to determine which performs better, typically by measuring user engagement or conversion rates. This involves experimenting with different elements of email campaigns, such as subject lines, content, images, and CTAs, to identify what resonates best with the audience. A/B testing allows for data-driven decisions, refining email strategies for optimal engagement and conversions.

Personalization Beyond the Name

While addressing subscribers by their name is a common personalization tactic, true personalization in email marketing goes beyond salutations. Entrepreneurs navigate the landscape of personalization by tailoring content based on subscriber preferences, behaviors, and purchase history.

Dynamic content that adapts to individual preferences enhances the relevance of email communication.

Measuring Key Metrics for Success

Navigating the landscape of email marketing involves analyzing key metrics to gauge the success of campaigns. Entrepreneurs monitor metrics such as open rates, click-through rates, conversion rates, and unsubscribe rates. These metrics provide valuable insights into subscriber engagement and campaign effectiveness, guiding adjustments for future campaigns.

Compliance with Regulations

In the landscape of email marketing, compliance with regulations such as the General Data Protection Regulation (GDPR) in the European Union and the CAN-SPAM Act in the United States is non-negotiable. Entrepreneurs must navigate the landscape of legal and ethical considerations to ensure that their email marketing practices adhere to privacy laws, protecting both the brand and the trust of subscribers.

Nurturing Long-Term Customer Relationships

Beyond driving immediate conversions, email marketing excels in nurturing long-term customer relationships. Entrepreneurs navigate the landscape of relationship-building by delivering consistent value, maintaining open communication, and adapting email strategies based on evolving customer preferences. Building trust through email communication contributes to customer loyalty and lifetime value.

Conclusion

Email marketing mastery is an artful blend of strategy, creativity, and responsiveness to the ever-evolving digital landscape. Entrepreneurs navigate the landscape of email marketing by building engaged subscriber lists, segmenting for personalized communication, crafting compelling content, and utilizing automation for timely messaging. Success in email marketing requires a commitment to optimization, personalization, compliance with regulations, and, above all, the cultivation of enduring customer relationships. In the realm of Entrepreneurship in the Digital Landscape, email marketing emerges not just as a promotional channel but as a transformative force that delicately nurtures connections, fosters brand loyalty, and drives sustained business success.

Introduction

In the dynamic landscape of Entrepreneurship in the Digital Era, the ability to communicate effectively is a cornerstone of success. Public speaking, often underestimated, is a skill that can elevate entrepreneurs by enhancing their personal and professional growth. This article explores the art of public speaking for entrepreneurs, guiding them on honing this skill to leave a lasting impact in the digital landscape.

Recognizing the Importance of Public Speaking

Public speaking is more than standing in front of an audience; it's a strategic tool that allows entrepreneurs to convey their ideas, influence others, and build connections. Navigating the landscape of entrepreneurship in the digital era involves recognizing the importance of public speaking as a means to communicate effectively in various contexts.

Building Confidence

Confidence is the bedrock of effective public speaking. Entrepreneurs navigate the landscape of building confidence by understanding their content thoroughly, practicing regularly, and adopting techniques to manage nervousness. Confidence not only enhances the delivery of a message but also captivates the audience and fosters trust.

Crafting and Refining Your Message

Navigating the landscape of public speaking requires entrepreneurs to carefully craft and refine their messages. Clear and concise messaging is essential for capturing the audience's attention and ensuring that key points are conveyed effectively. Entrepreneurs should focus on creating messages that resonate with their audience and align with their brand identity.

Understanding Your Audience

Successful public speaking involves understanding the audience and tailoring the message accordingly. Entrepreneurs navigate the landscape of audience understanding by researching their demographics, interests, and preferences. This knowledge allows them to connect with the audience on a deeper level, making the message more relatable and impactful.

Effective Body Language

Body language is a powerful component of public speaking. Entrepreneurs navigate the landscape of body language by maintaining good posture, making eye contact, and using gestures purposefully. Positive body language not only reinforces the spoken message but also conveys confidence and credibility to the audience.

Utilizing Vocal Variety

The vocal tone and delivery style significantly impact the effectiveness of a speech. Entrepreneurs navigate the landscape of vocal variety by modulating their tone, pace, and pitch to keep the audience engaged. A varied and expressive voice adds dynamism to the presentation, preventing monotony and enhancing the overall impact.

Engaging the Audience

Public speaking is a two-way communication process. Entrepreneurs navigate the landscape of audience engagement by incorporating interactive elements such as questions, anecdotes, and real-world examples. Engaging the audience fosters a connection and ensures that the message resonates beyond the spoken words.

Utilizing Visual Aids

In the digital landscape, visual aids can enhance the impact of a presentation. Entrepreneurs navigate the landscape of visual aids by incorporating slides, images, and videos that complement their message. Well-designed visuals not only support key points but also cater to different learning styles, making the content more accessible.

Practicing Effective Time Management

Time is a precious resource, and effective public speaking involves navigating the landscape of time management. Entrepreneurs practice and refine their speeches to fit within allocated time frames. Well-managed time ensures that key points are covered without rushing and helps maintain the audience's attention throughout the presentation.

Handling Q&A Sessions with Grace

Q&A sessions are an integral part of public speaking engagements. Entrepreneurs navigate the landscape of Q&A sessions by preparing for potential questions, responding with clarity and composure, and embracing questions as an opportunity to deepen audience engagement. Skillful handling of Q&A sessions builds credibility and reinforces the speaker's expertise.

Leveraging Digital Platforms for Virtual Speaking

In the digital era, public speaking extends beyond physical stages to virtual platforms. Entrepreneurs navigate the landscape of virtual speaking by leveraging video conferencing tools, webinars, and online events. Adapting to the nuances of virtual communication is essential for reaching and influencing a global audience.

Seeking Feedback for Continuous Improvement

Continuous improvement is the hallmark of effective public speaking. Entrepreneurs navigate the landscape of improvement by seeking constructive feedback from peers, mentors, or audience members. Actively incorporating feedback allows entrepreneurs to refine their speaking skills, address areas of improvement, and grow as communicators.

Conclusion

Public speaking is a skill that empowers entrepreneurs to amplify their personal and professional growth in the digital landscape of Entrepreneurship. By building confidence, crafting compelling messages, understanding the audience, and mastering essential techniques, entrepreneurs can navigate the landscape of public speaking with finesse. In an era where effective communication is paramount, the ability to speak with impact not only sets entrepreneurs apart but also enables them to influence, inspire, and leave a lasting imprint in the ever-evolving world of Entrepreneurship in the Digital Landscape.

Introduction

In the dynamic landscape of Entrepreneurship in the Digital Era, a comprehensive and well-crafted digital marketing plan is the compass that guides businesses toward success. This article explores the pivotal role of a Digital Marketing Planner, emphasizing the importance of strategic planning in the realm of digital marketing and providing a framework for entrepreneurs to create effective campaigns.

Understanding the Digital Marketing Landscape

Navigating the digital marketing landscape involves recognizing its multifaceted nature. Entrepreneurs must understand the diverse channels available, including social media, search engine optimization (SEO), content marketing, email marketing, and paid advertising. Acknowledging the breadth of options sets the stage for an effective digital marketing plan.

Setting Clear Business Objectives

A Digital Marketing Planner begins with a clear understanding of business objectives. Entrepreneurs navigate the landscape of goal-setting by defining specific, measurable, achievable, relevant, and time-bound (SMART) objectives. These objectives serve as the foundation upon which digital marketing strategies are built, aligning marketing efforts with overarching business goals.

Identifying Target Audiences

Successful digital marketing hinges on knowing the target audience intimately. Entrepreneurs navigate the landscape of audience identification by creating detailed buyer personas. These personas encompass demographic information, preferences, challenges, and behaviors, enabling businesses to tailor their digital marketing strategies to resonate with specific audience segments.

Conducting a Comprehensive SWOT Analysis

A Digital Marketing Planner requires a thorough analysis of the business's strengths, weaknesses, opportunities, and threats (SWOT). Entrepreneurs navigate the landscape of SWOT analysis to identify internal and external factors that impact their digital marketing efforts. Understanding these factors positions businesses to leverage strengths, address weaknesses, capitalize on opportunities, and mitigate threats.

Choosing the Right Digital Marketing Channels

Navigating the landscape of digital marketing involves selecting the most suitable channels to reach the target audience. Entrepreneurs assess the strengths of each channel - be it social media, SEO, content marketing, or paid advertising - and align their choices with the preferences and behaviors of their audience. An effective Digital Marketing Planner prioritizes channels that maximize reach and engagement.

Crafting a Content Strategy

Content is the backbone of digital marketing success. Entrepreneurs navigate the landscape of content strategy by creating a plan that aligns with business objectives and resonates with the target audience. A well-defined content strategy encompasses blog posts, articles, videos, infographics (visual representations of information or data designed to present complex concepts or data sets in a clear and easily understandable format), and other formats tailored to each digital marketing channel.

Implementing Search Engine Optimization (SEO) Strategies

In the digital landscape, visibility on search engines is paramount. Entrepreneurs navigate the landscape of SEO by optimizing their website, content, and online presence to rank higher on search engine results pages. Effective SEO strategies involve keyword research, on-page optimization, backlink building, and staying abreast of search engine algorithms.

Leveraging Social Media Marketing

Social media is a dynamic and influential channel in digital marketing. Entrepreneurs navigate the landscape of social media marketing by choosing platforms aligned with their target audience. Crafting a social media strategy involves creating engaging content, fostering community engagement, and leveraging paid advertising to amplify reach.

Email Marketing Excellence

Email marketing remains a potent tool for engaging and nurturing leads. Entrepreneurs navigate the landscape of email marketing by developing personalized and segmented campaigns. An effective email marketing strategy involves crafting compelling content, optimizing for mobile devices, and utilizing automation for targeted communication.

Paid Advertising Campaigns

Paid advertising is a strategic element of digital marketing. Entrepreneurs navigate the landscape of paid advertising by choosing platforms such as Google Ads, Facebook Ads, or LinkedIn Ads. Crafting effective paid advertising campaigns involves defining clear objectives, targeting the right audience, creating compelling ad creatives, and continuously optimizing for performance.

Implementing Analytics and Measurement Tools

An integral part of the Digital Marketing Planner is the incorporation of analytics and measurement tools. Entrepreneurs navigate the landscape of data by using tools such as Google Analytics to track the performance of their campaigns. Measuring key metrics, including website traffic, conversion rates, and engagement, provides valuable insights for refining strategies.

Iterative Improvement through Continuous Learning

The digital landscape is dynamic, requiring continuous adaptation. Entrepreneurs navigate the landscape of digital marketing by embracing a mindset of continuous learning. Staying informed about industry trends, algorithm updates, and emerging technologies ensures that digital marketing strategies remain effective and aligned with the evolving landscape.

Conclusion

The Digital Marketing Planner is a strategic blueprint that empowers entrepreneurs to navigate the complex terrain of digital marketing with purpose and precision. By setting clear objectives, identifying target audiences, conducting comprehensive analyses, choosing the right channels, and implementing effective strategies, entrepreneurs can maximize the impact of their digital marketing efforts. In the ever-evolving landscape of Entrepreneurship in the Digital Era, a well-crafted Digital Marketing Planner is not just a guide - it's a dynamic tool that propels businesses toward sustained growth, engagement, and success.

Chapter 14. Challenges and Innovations in Online Marketing

Introduction

In the ever-evolving landscape of Entrepreneurship in the Digital Era, online marketing plays a pivotal role in connecting businesses with their target audiences. However, this dynamic field is not without its challenges. This article explores the current challenges faced by online marketers and entrepreneurs and delves into the innovative solutions and trends shaping the future of online marketing.

Saturation and Intense Competition

Challenge: One of the primary challenges in online marketing is the saturation and intense competition across various industries. With numerous businesses vying for the attention of the same audience, standing out becomes increasingly challenging.

Innovation: Entrepreneurs are exploring niche marketing strategies to differentiate themselves. By targeting specific, underserved segments of the market, businesses can create tailored messages and offerings that resonate more deeply with their audience.

Ad-Blocking and Privacy Concerns

Challenge: The rise of ad-blockers and growing privacy concerns pose challenges for online marketers. As users become more conscious of their online privacy, traditional advertising methods face resistance.

Innovation: Personalized and permission-based marketing is gaining traction. Marketers are leveraging first-party data and user consent to deliver targeted content and ads. Transparency in data usage and emphasizing user control are key components of this innovative approach.

Algorithm Changes on Social Media Platforms

Challenge: Social media platforms frequently update their algorithms, affecting the organic reach of businesses. Algorithm changes can disrupt established marketing strategies and require constant adaptation.

Innovation: Diversification across multiple platforms helps mitigate the impact of algorithm changes on any single channel. Additionally, marketers are focusing on creating high-quality, engaging content that aligns with the platform's goals, increasing the likelihood of visibility.

Dynamic Search Engine Algorithms

Challenge: Search engines continuously refine their algorithms, impacting website rankings. Staying abreast of these changes and optimizing for search engines is an ongoing challenge for online marketers.

Innovation: Marketers are adopting a holistic approach to SEO that goes beyond traditional keyword optimization. This includes prioritizing user experience, creating high-quality content, and leveraging technical SEO to ensure websites align with search engine algorithms.

Short Attention Spans and Information Overload

Challenge: Consumers today face information overload and have shorter attention spans, making it challenging for marketers to capture and maintain their attention.

Innovation: Visual and interactive content is gaining prominence. Short-form videos, infographics, and interactive experiences cater to the preference for quick, engaging content. Marketers are focusing on creating visually appealing and snackable content to capture audience attention.

Rapid Technological Advancements

Challenge: While technology provides opportunities, it also poses challenges as it evolves rapidly. Keeping up with emerging technologies and understanding how to integrate them into marketing strategies can be daunting.

Innovation: Embracing marketing technology (MarTech) solutions is crucial. MarTech encompasses the tools, platforms, and software that marketers use to plan, execute, and analyze marketing campaigns and activities, leveraging technology to streamline processes and enhance overall effectiveness. Automation, artificial intelligence, and data analytics are revolutionizing marketing. Entrepreneurs are investing in MarTech tools to streamline processes, gain insights, and stay ahead in the competitive landscape.

Evolving Consumer Expectations

Challenge: Consumer expectations are evolving, demanding personalized and seamless experiences across all touchpoints. Meeting these expectations requires a deep understanding of consumer behavior.

Innovation: Hyper-personalization is at the forefront of addressing evolving expectations. Utilizing customer data, AI-driven personalization engines can deliver tailored experiences, recommendations, and content, enhancing customer satisfaction and loyalty.

Global Economic Uncertainties

Challenge: Economic uncertainties on a global scale, as seen in events like the COVID-19 pandemic, can significantly impact consumer behavior, purchasing power, and overall market conditions.

Innovation: Agile marketing strategies that allow quick adaptation to changing circumstances are essential. Entrepreneurs are diversifying their offerings, exploring new markets, and leveraging digital channels to stay resilient in the face of economic uncertainties.

Inclusivity and Diversity in Marketing

Challenge: Consumers are increasingly seeking brands that demonstrate inclusivity and diversity. Inclusivity and diversity refer to the practice and commitment of creating environments, policies, and cultures that embrace and respect individuals of various backgrounds, experiences, identities, and perspectives, fostering a sense of belonging and equal opportunities for everyone. Failing to address these concerns can lead to a loss of trust and credibility.

Innovation: Inclusive marketing that represents diverse voices and perspectives is becoming a norm. Entrepreneurs are actively incorporating inclusivity into their brand messaging, advertising campaigns, and overall company culture to resonate with a broader audience.

Measuring Return on Investment (ROI)

Challenge: Return on Investment (ROI) is a key performance indicator used to measure the effectiveness and profitability of digital marketing efforts. It involves assessing the financial returns generated from online marketing activities relative to the costs incurred. Determining the ROI of online marketing efforts can be complex due to the multitude of channels and touchpoints involved in the customer journey.

Innovation: Advanced analytics and attribution models are helping marketers better measure and attribute the impact of each marketing channel. By leveraging data-driven insights, businesses can optimize their marketing mix for maximum ROI.

Conclusion

In the digital landscape of Entrepreneurship, challenges and innovations go hand in hand. Entrepreneurs and online marketers must navigate the dynamic landscape by embracing innovative solutions to address saturation, privacy concerns, algorithm changes, and other obstacles. By staying informed, adopting new technologies, and prioritizing consumer-centric approaches, businesses can not only overcome challenges but also thrive in the digital era. As the digital landscape continues to evolve, the ability to adapt and innovate will be the cornerstone of success for entrepreneurs in the intricate world of online marketing.

Chapter 15. The Future of Entrepreneurship and Digital Marketing

Introduction

As we reach the culmination of "Entrepreneurship in the Digital Landscape", it's crucial to cast our gaze toward the future - anticipating the trends, challenges, and possibilities that will shape the world of entrepreneurship and digital marketing. The ever-evolving digital landscape presents both opportunities and complexities, requiring entrepreneurs to stay agile and innovative in their approach. In this final chapter, we explore the future of entrepreneurship, online marketing, and SEO, envisioning the path ahead.

Rise of Sustainable and Purpose-Driven Entrepreneurship

Anticipation: The future of entrepreneurship is expected to be increasingly driven by sustainability and purpose. Consumers are becoming more conscious, seeking businesses that align with their values and contribute positively to society and the environment.

Insight: Entrepreneurs embracing sustainability in their business practices, from eco-friendly products to ethical supply chains, will likely resonate strongly with the conscious consumer of the future. Purpose-driven entrepreneurship not only builds brand loyalty but also addresses pressing global challenges.

Integration of Augmented Reality (AR) and Virtual Reality (VR)

Augmented Reality (AR) overlays digital information onto the real-world environment, enhancing the user's perception of reality, while Virtual Reality (VR) immerses users in a computer-generated environment, completely replacing the real world with a simulated one.

Anticipation: The immersive experiences offered by AR and VR technologies are poised to revolutionize how consumers interact with brands. The future may see a seamless integration of these technologies into marketing strategies, providing customers with unique and engaging experiences.

Insight: Entrepreneurs willing to invest in AR and VR applications can create interactive campaigns, allowing customers to visualize products, engage in virtual try-ons, and participate in immersive brand experiences. This technology has the potential to elevate online shopping and brand engagement to new heights.

Artificial Intelligence (AI) as a Marketing Ally

Artificial Intelligence (AI) refers to the development of computer systems capable of performing tasks that typically require human intelligence, such as learning, reasoning, problem-solving, and decision-making.

Anticipation: AI is set to play a more significant role in marketing strategies, from personalized content recommendations to chatbots providing real-time customer support. The future holds the promise of AI-driven insights and automation, enhancing efficiency and customer experiences.

Insight: Entrepreneurs integrating AI into their digital marketing efforts can leverage data-driven decision-making, enabling more precise targeting and personalized interactions. AI-driven automation will streamline processes, allowing businesses to focus on creativity and strategy.

Voice Search Optimization in SEO

Voice search involves using spoken language to initiate an online search, utilizing voice recognition technology to interpret and respond to user queries, often through voice-activated devices or virtual assistants.

Anticipation: With the increasing popularity of voice-activated devices, voice search is becoming a dominant way users seek information. The future of SEO will see a shift toward optimizing content for voice search, emphasizing conversational keywords and context.

Insight: Entrepreneurs need to adapt their SEO strategies to accommodate the rise of voice search. This includes understanding natural language queries, optimizing for local search, and ensuring content is structured for featured snippets, which often power voice search results.

Blockchain Technology for Trust and Transparency

Blockchain technology is a decentralized and distributed ledger system that securely records and verifies transactions across multiple computers, ensuring transparency, immutability, and resistance to tampering, commonly associated with cryptocurrencies like Bitcoin.

Anticipation: Blockchain technology has the potential to reshape how businesses operate, emphasizing trust, transparency, and security. The future may witness blockchain applications in supply chain management, customer data protection, and secure online transactions.

Insight: Entrepreneurs adopting blockchain solutions can build trust with consumers by ensuring the integrity and security of their data. Blockchain's decentralized nature offers opportunities for creating transparent and tamper-proof systems, fostering credibility.

Ephemeral Content and the Rise of Short-Form Video

Anticipation: The popularity of ephemeral content, like stories on platforms such as Instagram and Snapchat, indicates a growing preference for short-form, easily digestible content. The future may see an increased reliance on these formats for marketing and brand communication.

Insight: Entrepreneurs should consider integrating short-form video content into their marketing strategies, leveraging platforms that emphasize ephemeral content. This approach caters to the shorter attention spans of modern consumers and fosters real-time, authentic connections with the audience.

Personalization 2.0: Hyper-Individualized Marketing

Anticipation: The future of digital marketing will move beyond generic personalization to hyper-individualized marketing. Advanced AI algorithms and data analytics will enable businesses to deliver content and experiences tailored to each user's unique preferences and behaviors.

Insight: Entrepreneurs investing in cutting-edge personalization technologies can create highly targeted and relevant marketing campaigns. By understanding individual consumer journeys, businesses can foster deeper connections and increase the likelihood of conversion.

The Evolution of Influencer Marketing

Influencer marketing is a strategy that involves collaborating with individuals, known as influencers, who have a significant and engaged following on social media platforms or other online channels, to promote a brand, product, or service to their audience.

Anticipation: Influencer marketing is likely to evolve, with a shift toward micro and nano influencers who have smaller but highly engaged audiences. The future may see a more authentic and relatable approach, as consumers value genuine connections with influencers.

Insight: Entrepreneurs collaborating with micro and nano influencers can tap into niche communities and build authentic brand advocates. Focusing on genuine connections rather than just follower count will likely be more impactful in the evolving landscape of influencer marketing.

Continued Emphasis on Content Quality

Anticipation: While the formats may change, the importance of high-quality content will remain a constant in digital marketing. The future will demand content that not only engages but also adds value, resonating with the audience on a deeper level.

: Entrepreneurs should prioritize content creation that aligns with their brand narrative, addresses audience needs, and stands out in a saturated digital landscape. Investing in storytelling, educational content, and multimedia experiences will be key.

Environmental and Ethical E-Commerce Practices

Environmental and ethical e-commerce practices involve conducting online business operations in a manner that minimizes negative impacts on the environment and upholds ethical standards. This can include various initiatives and considerations such as sustainable sourcing, reducing packaging waste, carbon neutrality, transparency and fair labor practices, ethical marketing, product longevity and repairability, social responsibility, customer education, green hosting and technology, and recycling programs. By integrating these practices, e-commerce businesses can contribute to environmental sustainability, uphold ethical standards, and meet the growing demand from consumers who prioritize socially responsible and eco-friendly choices.

Anticipation: E-commerce practices are expected to evolve with a heightened emphasis on environmental and ethical considerations. The future may see consumers favoring businesses that adopt sustainable practices in packaging, shipping, and overall operations.

Insight: Entrepreneurs incorporating eco-friendly and ethical practices into their e-commerce models can appeal to a growing segment of environmentally conscious consumers. Transparency in sourcing, sustainable packaging, and responsible supply chain management will be pivotal.

Conclusion

As we conclude our exploration of "Entrepreneurship in the Digital Landscape", it's evident that the future holds exciting opportunities and challenges. Entrepreneurs navigating tomorrow's landscape must embrace sustainability, leverage emerging technologies, and prioritize authentic connections with their audience. From the integration of AR and VR to the rise of hyper-personalization, the entrepreneurial journey in the digital era is bound to be dynamic, requiring adaptability and a forward-thinking mindset. As we step into the future, let this be a reminder that the landscape may change, but the core principles of innovation, authenticity, and a customer-centric approach will continue to be the guiding stars for entrepreneurial success in the digital realm.

"Entrepreneurship in the Digital Landscape" is a comprehensive exploration of the intricate relationship between entrepreneurship and the digital era. It begins by unraveling the journey of first-generation entrepreneurs, shedding light on the unique challenges and opportunities inherent in pioneering family enterprises. The book delves into the distinctive mindset that distinguishes successful entrepreneurs in the digital age, emphasizing qualities crucial for navigating the evolving business landscape. As the narrative unfolds, the intersection of entrepreneurship and the digital realm is dissected, highlighting the paramount importance of adaptability in this dynamic environment.

Readers are guided through the landscape of online business, witnessing the transformative role of digital marketing. From the historical evolution of online marketing to strategies for crafting a robust digital presence, the book covers diverse aspects, including SEO fundamentals, social media marketing nuances, and the influential art of content marketing. It further explores email marketing, public speaking for entrepreneurs, and the significance of strategic planning in digital marketing campaigns. The book concludes by addressing current challenges, exploring innovative solutions, and speculating on future trends in entrepreneurship, online marketing, and SEO. This comprehensive guide is an invaluable resource for both aspiring and seasoned entrepreneurs navigating the complexities of the digital landscape.

ABOUT THE AUTHOR

Mr. C. P. Kumar is a retired Scientist 'G' from National Institute of Hydrology, Roorkee, Uttarakhand, India. He is also a Reiki Healer and Chakra Balancing practitioner (with pendulum dowsing) and offers Emotional Freedom Technique (EFT) to help individuals with emotional issues. Mr. Kumar has authored many books on technical, spiritual, and social topics.

For further details, you may visit his webpage
https://www.angelfire.com/nh/cpkumar/virgo.html